Sky Burials

SKY BURIALS

Ben Smith

First published in 2014 by
Worple Press
Achill Sound, 2b Dry Hill Road
Tonbridge
Kent TN9 1LX.
www.worplepress.co.uk

Cover image by Max Smith

Printed by imprintdigital
Upton Pyne, Exeter
www.imprintdigital.net

Typeset by narrator
www.narrator.me.uk
info@narrator.me.uk
033 022 300 39

ISBN: 978-1-905208-29-6

Acknowledgements

Grateful acknowledgements are due to the editors of the following publications, where some of these poems first appeared: *Agenda* ('St. Ronan's Chapel' and 'The Stone Boats of the Saints'), *Canto* ('Magpie Words' and 'Ordinary Surface Birds'), *Earthlines* ('Augury with Rubber Ducks' and 'Black Swans'), *Entanglements: New Ecopoetry* (*'from* Lessons in Augury'), *Envoi* ('Sky Burial' and 'Unidentified Bones') and *The London Magazine* ('The Wolves of Chernobyl').

Thanks to Peter and Amanda Carpenter; to Andy Brown for a decade of teaching, advice and friendship; to Jos Smith, Miriam Darlington, Philip Gross and Eleanor Rees for reading and supporting my work; and to Lucy, for everything.

Contents

Augury with Rubber Ducks

In 1992 a container of 28,800 rubber ducks was lost at sea. Most of them are still out there…

Teach us of the roulette wheel of storms,
of gyre systems, tide systems, the strange currents
that we have heard are brewing out at sea.
Teach us of life beyond shipping lanes, of movement
shaped by water, of seams worn thin by water,
of fathoms seen through painted eyes.

And, years from now, when you arrive on scattered beaches
teach us of the ice that locked you in for lifetimes,
repackaging you as bright yellow sediment.
Teach us how you shrugged the ice-melt from your backs
as you rejoined the rising water, the unknown patterns of water.
Teach us of endurance. Remember us

as you navigate the empty shipping lanes, the new geographies
of plastic that we left gathering, gathering.

The Weather Station

Beneath the dishes on the cliffs, they are mapping a future world.
Tide-systems and cloud-formations bloom across the screens.
In one corner, a pot plant blooms
beneath the glow of an ultraviolet lamp.
They have been here for years, in these airless rooms,
measuring, blinking, watching changes unfold like ferns.

Their own lives passed in a breath. They do not think of them.
They have seen stone turn to liquid, liquid to stone,
mountains burst in the ground like seeds
and valleys open, close, to a deeper, tectonic breathing.

Their maps breathe and grow. Screens flicker.
The pot plant dies. Someone replaces it.
The room shakes then stills,
the floor splits and ice blooms on their cuffs and collars.
They stumble on the broken edges of continents,
their footsteps disappearing behind them.

They have seen it. There is nothing to do
but watch, blink, measure

and yet, some nights they go out to the cliffs
to draw lots beneath the pale moons of the dishes.
One steps forward – you can see him through the wire –
wearing rags? No, feathers…

and as he jumps from the cliffs, graceful and silent,
you can hear their prayer:
that before he hits the surf, he will rise as a bird
and bring a change in the weather.

St Peter and the Storm Petrels

Footsteps on water.

Dawn clear as prayer.
Bodies hanging over water

like small, dark beads.

How long have they been out there
treading slowly across the bay,
staring down into the salt-clear distances,
scrying for storms?

There was a time when a saint walked on water.
We saw him – a bright light crossing the bay
leaving a trail of taut, still water
marked with footprints.

He left long ago, turning west
on his weightless march,
leaning into the heft of the waves
like a restless ship.

We still wait for him to return,
but perhaps, lost or driven mad
by such winds, such distances,
this is what he has become –

a petrel hanging over water,
staring down as if in wonder
and pattering its ragged dance

to the distant, scudding footfall of storms.

Oystercatchers

Down among the mussel beds
the water is warming by degrees.

One by one
            we drift down
                        from the cliffs
to huddle on the mussel beds
and by degrees
            to change.

Our heads fill with watery thoughts
the flexing of tides
                  the soft clack of shells.

And, like shells, our beaks clack and grow,
broadening
            hardening
                        layer on layer;

like the sand
            re-layered over winter
into new drifts and pebble beds;

like the pebbles
                  turned hard and smooth
by the water's endless turning.

The Stone Boats of the Saints

We need no wind for our stone boats,
we don't need to wait for the tide.
We need no canvas, no pitch, no rope,
no benches, no ballast, no oars.
We need no tools for our stone boats,
they are already there, on the sandless shore –
black granite hulls among the limestone's grey angles
like weights and measures
left over from the workings of the world.

We are searching for beginnings –
thumb-prints on the cliffs, the first sketches
of islands beyond the rim of the sea.
We have no charts to find our way.
We need no moon, no stars,
just our stone boats seeking out fellow stone.
We haul them into the slate-grey waters.
Our path lies ahead of us, bright as a seam of quartz.

Black Swans

Noun (meteorological): freak weather events, less rare than previously thought.

At first, no one believed it – a hiss
of rain that grew into pounding flight.
Roads and fields swept away by wings. Power lines
dragged down by thrashing wings.

More story than bulk and weight, we half-forgot it
(but still shuddered at thrown shadows, rugs being beaten for dust).
We moved on. We rebuilt the roads.
And no one noticed the feathers in the cooling tarmac,
the creak of wings like the echo of trees,

until swans filled the sky, beaching their dark hulls
over fields, smothering new shoots in snow,
smothering roofs,
snapping water pipes and bridges like limbs.

Now, droughts and wild-fires spread in wingspans,
hurricanes lumber towards water

and deep in the sea an oil pipe bursts.
We do not mistake the dark shape billowing,
hauling itself through currents, shedding feathers
but still gaining mass, growing
by Richters, by seismic shifts.

Flood Spiders

When the waters rose, the spiders rose like smoke
into the trees.
                         The trees like snuffed candles
punctuated the flood plain.
                                      The flood plain dimmed
to deep water.

The rain came sudden as an eclipse. In windows
and doorways children watched drops the size of light bulbs
darken the broken soil.
                              Inside, adults gathered
what could be carried to higher ground.

Outside, the spiders rose through the rain.

They began lightly, joining twig to twig
branch to branch
                           then spooling whole trees
in darkening thread
until the trees swelled and warped like half-filled balloons.
The spiders tightened their threads

as a wind troubled the surface of the water
and, one by one, the trees untethered from their roots
and rose into the sky.
                              From the hills, the people watched
the emptiness of water.
In the sky, the spiders slackened and flexed their threads,
guiding their vessels towards the horizon.

Sea Augury

Here, at the furthest point from land
we pitch containers from the deck

like dice the size of houses
and wait to see what rises as the water stills.

We follow the cargo shoaling in the currents
the way the first sailors followed wooden pillars

to the beaches of their new worlds.
We wade ashore across a tide line of disposable watches,

plastic bags tugging at the shallows
like tired moons.

Turnstones

We continue the water's work, levering the damp corners

of pebbles, working the shoreline – light to dark

light to dark – until sandhoppers scatter like light through water

or we find something more worth our working.

We are proficient with eggs and bars of soap, all kinds of waste.

We can dispose of bodies – wearing down skin

wearing down bone – until, like us, they disappear

into the wrack line. You can't tell where

our movement finishes and the water's begins.

Ordinary Surface Birds

'We are plain, ordinary surface birds'
                                        — *Skaay.*

Out to sea, the gannets fall like heavy, slanting rain;
disappearing like water into water.
I wait for them to rise again

like bubbles
hanging on the surface, pausing
as they readjust to the bulk and noise of air.

I try to guess how long they will be under
and what they'll see, crossing from weightlessness
into weightlessness,

what visions they will return with
in the oily sheen of their feathers.
But here, on the cliffs, the rain begins to fall

like gannets,
                like guillemots
                                and terns.

And all I can see, beyond the whitening cliffs,
are the hard flashes of beaks and wing-tips
breaking through the clouds.

Dipper

Strange, finding a voice down here
among pebbles and the pull of water.

I duck under,
shouldering the river's weight.

Strange, this dark curled thing, darting
through the shadows of the river bed
into the coils of a water-snail's shell.

I grab it, bring it to the surface,
unfurl it in the empty air.

St Ronan's Chapel

The stones give no answers.
Cracks in the mortar admit only threads of sky.
Stone bench,
stone altar;
if there were books they would be bound in stone.

No sound finds its way down the long, low tunnel
to shelter from the wind –
not the storm petrel's lost-soul laughter,
not the seal's soft wailing
stretching over the surrounding waters.

All we know is that *Ronan* means *little seal*,
as though one of those creatures,
wondering at the new shapes crossing
the straits, the lights on distant cliffs,
rose one day and walked inland,

shedding blubber and fur in the milk-white shallows,
taking a new skin of rough cloth
washed ashore in a storm.
And perhaps this darkness and silence
is not the result of a person's search for wilderness,

but an attempt by something wild
to turn its back on the light of the sky
and the clamour of the waves,
to see its world through our eyes,
hear it through our ears.

Magpie Words

Was it in the speckle-shelled before
that the devil spliced a thread of his blood
with the first inkling of who we are?
Or was it during that first hungry yawn
that he slipped in, as insect or grub,
and grazed our throats with song?
I do not know, but I know that my love
for brightness comes from a darkness
in my gut, where consonants chatter
and knot together, and vowels gape
like empty nests.
I know that when I creep in to crack
a hoard of shining eggs,
I can already taste a bitter drop of blood,
like the beginnings of a word,
pooling in the curve of my tongue.

Nightbird Riddles

Barn Owl

Follow me, your pilot light –
a single bulb left swinging over fields.

Step into the grip and weight
of my orbit. The silent pressure

of my wings can ward off storms.
Don't be afraid. Even in this deep wood

I glow from hollow trees.
Step inside.

Where your eyes fail,
follow the screeching hinge of my call.

Woodcock

Even by day I am invisible
so please tread carefully

as I do.

I never cross fallen logs,
I've memorized my zig-zag
flight path through the trees.

You should too.

I am neither bat nor frog.
You're cock-sure enough
to call me stupid;
but I know exactly where I am.

Do you?

Tawny Owl

Do you know where you are, or who
you can now hear?

I have already sounded out
several deaths tonight. To wit:

three mice, one stoat and a magpie who
strayed too close to my nest.

Just like you.

If you wish to speak, clasp your hands
as if in prayer or supplication.

I might look kindly
on the blind glint of your eyes.

from Lessons in Augury

Transcribed from recently discovered stone tablet fragments.
Origin: forgotten.
Date: unverified.

Lesson I: Introductions

Call me Attus Navius. Call me St. Francis of the Birds. Call me Calchas, Tiresias, Laocoon, St. Milburga or Cuthbert of Lindisfarne.

They say I was raised in an eyrie, that I have feathers under my coat. But they soon stop laughing when I see a peregrine stoop and send the whole country to war.

Do you see that kestrel – a marionette under the clouds? I can show you how to pull the right strings. Give me a pair of hungry rooks and I'll set brother against brother. Father against son. A well trained dove has won me the trust of bank managers and kings. When I send my pigeons out at night, they return heavy with people's gratitude (in blank envelopes please, in unmarked bills).

Call me Black Elk, Ten Bears, Don Juan Matus. Call me Mopsus, Lizard's Son, Skaay.

I've outlived every one of them and I'm better than them all combined. I can slip outside time like a pocket-watch in a forgotten magpie's nest, like water beading on a pintail's back.

I've seen other worlds appear in the curve of a starling's feather. I've watched other pasts, other futures, unfold like an albatross' wings. For the right price I can give you vision sharp as a talon. I can teach you how to unwind fate – easy as wringing a chicken's neck.

Lesson XVII: Defining Terms

Truth is a slippery term. Try to avoid it. Like the cliff ledges where fulmars rise suddenly to shoulder height, squinting at you and smiling their moon-faced smiles. Hang around too long and they'll spew in your face.

Certainty: no better. How can anything be certain when no one knows where storm petrels go for most of the year? Release one anywhere in the world and it'll fly straight back to where you snatched it. That's certainty! I've probed deep inside skulls – sand martins, arctic terns – searching for the iron filings, the hidden compasses. But there are just cavities and channels in the bone.

That's the future: all edges, precipices and sheer drops into nothing. Or is it edgeless as a marsh? Centreless as the echo of a bittern hunched and booming in the reeds? You could walk in circles for days, for years, and never find the nest. You could lose yourself. You could hide a body. What I'm trying to tell you is: what you're searching for is always on the other side of the drainage ditch.

No. Too vague. The future is like a feather – you can watch it fall or use it to line your quilt.

There used to be good months for feathers and eggs. Then I found a swallow's nest in November. The eggs cold in the damp moss and lichen. These are the seasons now: weaving back into each other like stalks of grass or clumping together like mud under the eaves. I don't remember when I stopped going outside.

Nature: that used to mean something didn't it? That was where we saw things. Where we heard things.

Signs. Yes, I remember. If someone wanted to pass a law, I'd find them a ribbon of geese in the right quarter of sky. If a government needed a shake up, I'd bring in a crow that could croak the right names. But now I just sit in my chair, scanning the blank square of the skylight. Waiting for something. For what?

Birds. Must we always talk of birds? What are they anyway? Little parcels of the future. I unravel them and sell the contents. And yet, the sky has never seemed so empty. Difficult to predict. But no matter. We always know what the Gods have in mind.

The Gods. Now we come to it. The Gods are, and always have been, the highest bidders.

Lesson XXIX: *Difficult Customers*

Everyone likes to think that their fate will be determined by an eagle with a snake in its talons emerging from a blood red sun. Try to temper their expectations. Their future is probably already taking shape, like the crooked mess of a jackdaw's nest in a chimney. Stick by stick. Hour by hour. The thump of dunnocks flying into closed windows, day after day.

Everyone likes to think that they'd notice it: the briefest of shadows passing over the sun, a flutter of blood suddenly stilled in the hedges, a single wing-beat – nothing more than a breath – cutting back against the wind. But they just button up their coats or fumble through their pockets, as if searching for their keys. Or find themselves, on starless nights, walking barefoot through fields of corn-stubble, waiting for dark feathers to fall from the sky.

Everyone thinks they can handle the truth; but it can be too much even for us. I knew a great seer who predicted how long he had left. When the day came and nothing happened, he laughed himself to death. I once had a client who couldn't take any more and put a gun to his head. I'd only got as far as explaining the gulls on the fence posts – he never even saw the pheasant on his roof, the line of geese walking in through his half-open door.

I'd like to think you'd be sensitive to the situation. If you foresee happiness and riches, it's best to be sure – book them in for regular readings, arrange a monthly payment plan. But if it all looks bad then tell them straight. Just ask for your fee in advance.

The Final Lesson: Retirement Plans

You'll know when it's time. You'll hear muttering in the corridors, like lengths of rope being uncoiled and cut to size. Scaffolding will appear and no one will tell you why. You'll hear popping on the phone line. Friends will stop returning your calls. Your letters will arrive days late, crinkled at the edges, re-sealed with glue. When you reach the back door of the minister's offices, someone will have changed the locks.

Don't let them know that you know. Carry on as usual. Make plans for the coming weeks. Even better, let them think you're losing it. Go out with no socks. Stand all day at the end of your street, mouth open, staring at the sky. Then one night, just leave. Tell no one. Take what you need from your locker at the bus station, your box buried in the allotments. Send anything you have to the newspapers – stolen files, diaries, taped meetings.

Pick a direction and walk. Walk until you reach the mountains. Walk until you reach the sea. Walk until you reach the house that you bought long ago and have kept under a different name. Sleep with your money under your mattress, broken egg shells round your bed. Wake early. Watch the skies. Watch until the gulls flying over are nothing but gulls, the pigeons in the fields nothing but an easy meal.

Wait, like the last time this happened.

Over the horizon, cities will rise and fall. Like the tides. Like the leaves falling from the hedges. Like the birds returning, year after year, until one cold bright day they will bring new messages, like voices over the radio suddenly clear after a long night lost in static.

Derangements of Scale

'Environmental slogans follow horrifying predictions of climate chaos with injunctions, no less solemn, not to leave electrical appliances on standby or overfill the kettle. Such language enacts a bizarre derangement of scales, collapsing the trivial and the catastrophic into each other'

— *Timothy Clark*

I boil the kettle and the crow is back at the window.
This has happened before. Maybe it has always happened.
I used to know a thing about birds – something
about feeding habits, something about patterns of flight –
but from here this crow looks the size of a tower block.
He walks the length of the horizon, staring at himself in the glass.

I boil the kettle and a tower block falls. It's okay,
I knew that this would happen. There were signs
in the newspapers and pasted to lamp-posts.
But I didn't know that the sky would fill with dust;
that the roof-tops, the window, the crow,
would all turn white with dust. I do not know
why the crow is collecting coat hangers, tangles of wire.

I boil the kettle and the TV loses itself in a storm. There is no news,
but if I listen at the wall I can hear talk of the weather –
that it will get much hotter, that it will get much colder.
I still have power, but across the street, lights disappear,
as if the crow is stretching his wings.

At night, the kettle switches on. I wake
to the sound of flood waters, of foundations murmuring.
I turn over. At least I don't need to worry about the kettle any more.

Through the wall, in the kitchen and in kitchens across the city,
water pools in rows of untouched cups
and crows rise like heavy clouds of steam
lugging themselves towards open windows.

The Death of Calchas

A great seer predicted the date of his death. But these things rarely go as planned...

I rose early, washed and dressed, shaved
with a newly sharpened blade. The metal
dug into my skin like a spade, drew out
nothing but small red seeds.

I walked bare-legged among boulders
where vipers were coiled in the sun like springs.
But they didn't even twitch as I passed.

A sudden storm raged and I made my way
into the eye of it –
a small shape vanishing in turbulence and din.
But the wind shucked off me like a layer of dead skin.

And a tortoise fell from the sky
and missed me by metres.

And none of my enemies could get hold of any poison.

And even the mean back-streets were bustling.

And now, as the day buries itself in the sea
I know, for the first time, what it's like to be wrong.

Funny

how this laughter grips me,
like reassuring hands around my throat.

Odin's Ravens

There used to be just two, loosed at dawn
– like flinging a pair of shutters open –
to gather the news on the wind.

Now, a clamouring fog mobs him, gabbling
of every new twist in the knot of the world.
He stands on his mountain top, barely
has time to gather the loose rubble of his thoughts
before another is back, squabbling, fretting,
jostling for room.

Nothing but feathers, beaks,
the hot stench of bodies.
He can't remember when he stopped listening.

In the Everglades

Silence

of water. Silence

of small mammals and frogs.

Silence of deer, picking their way

through the shallows. Somewhere

something gathers the silences, coiling

them into bulk and length. There are trails

in the water, wide as dragged sacks of meat.

Once, one was found burst open –

a whole dead alligator sprung from its insides

like a steel trap.

But the trails are broader now and, at the end

of the day, all nets and snares are found

torn from their moorings. Silence

of foxes.   Silence of bobcat

and panther – deeper

than the usual silence.

Night closes over

the Everglades

swallowing

it whole.

The First Bear

And I saw, as it were, a white bear
crossing the dark edge of the town,
dragging a bin bag like a dead seal.
It moved silently, while the weight of its scent
silenced all dogs for miles.

It lingered, outshining the lights
of car parks and forecourts,
lost in the greys and browns of the world.

And I saw, as it were, not a bear
but the ghost of a bear
and the first of many,
gathering at the edge of the town
like the snow that hasn't fallen in living memory.

Unidentified Bones

All that they found of me:
three vertebrae,
                    the curve of a jaw,
a clutch of teeth and knuckles,
one rib, an inch of femur
sewn into the river.

I had already forgotten myself
when they sent divers
                        sieving through the murk.
My memories hang just below the surface
like air trapped in tin cans and jars.

    There was a young man with an average height
    and an approximate time of death –
    a figure sketched
                        from scrapings of bone marrow
    and the guesswork of a coroner's report.

I must have lost my way by the river.
The water filled my shoes with a sudden gulp

of cold and grit, before warming to my blood.
I let the current curl around my calves.
My skin was rasped away
on rocks, my nerves
                        unravelled over flood plains.

    The dredgers trawled the bed for days,

but I was knotted into willow roots,
braced inside the shafts of reeds.

Sometimes I dream of a body:

> a nest of bones wrapped in plastic,
> packed in a numbered box.

Sometimes I feel them
trying to piece me together –

> the cold metal tools,
> the sterile warmth
> of latex-gloved hands.

Archaeopteryx

Was I the first?
It never felt that way to me.
You found a single feather
or rather
        a feather-shaped absence
that you filled
          with scurrying lizards
splays of wings.

Soon, you were seeing dinosaurs
perched in your garden hedge.

And you want to put a label on me.

What is a bird anyway?
I've never seen one.

You look for answers, dusting
          round my outline;
but I'm a contortionist, wrapped
in the great chain of being,
        ready to wriggle free.

The Wolves of Chernobyl

You ask about the wolves. The reports are unclear,
but it is said that they are without number.
When they run the long, empty roads
it is as a dark rush of water.
When they reach the town they flood the streets,
stalk the bare rooms like shades. The hollow shells
of churches and train stations fill
with the heat of their breath.

You ask of their hunger, the strength of their jaws.
It is said that the forests are stripped of their bark,
that the graveyards are turned to churned earth,
splintered wood and bone.
It is said they are digging deep in the hills.
There is nothing to be done.

The wolves can sense all movement for miles.
No one walks near the fence at night.
Drivers keep their eyes on the road,
their windows wound up tight.
They know what bristling, breathing darkness
stalks beyond the headlights' arc, beyond
the singing wire.

But you ask about the wolves – what do they know?
It is said that they sit at the mouth of the mines
for days and nights,
staring into the flooded depths.

You ask about their eyes. There is nothing I can say.
They have gazed into the light at the end of the world,
then turned and walked away.

Sky Burial

I will become pollen

and sand

sheep's wool hooked on wire

thistle heads, torn roots of thrift

twigs and feathers

talons, beaks and feathers

silhouettes in the sea drenched air.

I will become cumulus and altostratus

cirrus and mackerel sky

troposphere, mesosphere, ionosphere

storm after storm

after storm